THE
ART OF THE
MIRROR

GEORGE D. PYRIOHOS

Ordering Information:

Prime Seven Media
518 Landmann St.
Tomah City, WI 54660

Printed in the United States of America

INTRODUCTION

You will probably think to yourselves that a topic like Psychoanalysis is complex issue to handle. Psychoanalysis has many factors. For starters it can be challenging. A challenge is always welcome. Once someone will get the hang of it, it will be a adventure. There will be a lot of things where someone can discover.

The human mind never stops working. Even in sleep, in a hiatus, in any state the mind works. It will think of the past, the present and even the future. A person can become vocal, but usually the person can be quiet in thought. The person could talk to himself and be heard, but usually you won't see that.

This is a search, in one way. It could be a recall of the past, the contemporary situation where that person is living in and there could be future planning. All of this silently or vocally. The main cause of these thoughts is the being of this person.

According to the way of thinking, this could lead somebody to the so called "good", if all things go well, and the "bad" if things go wrong. All of this is just relevant. Putting all of this in an order, has to do with the functioning of the mind.

All of this will be explained, or will tried to be explained here, firstly in a general context, then when being specific.

In the beginning this will seem to be vague. The issue will become clearer as we will continue.

Everyday situations can be handled in many ways. A person can go about going on to use psychoanalysis for some issue. It can be used as a "tool". Tools have to be used properly for the results to be effective.

We all have been lead to believe that when there is a reference to psychoanalysis, there is a depiction of Sigmund Freud, and of psychiatrists. For many people a psychiatrist can lead to a fear, as with many that will be afraid of the dentist, or of other medical professionals and hospitals, clinics and of the sort. We will be able to refer to fears that will be relevant.

The aim is to refer to methods that can be used in the quest of well being. This well being will have physical, psychological traits that may combine to influence each being.

When somebody will seek to do something, that person will always try to find the easy way of doing something, whether or not it is right or wrong. An example here is when we have sat for a test, an exam. You will see the studious that have studied for hours and the cheats trying to get about easier in such a situation. This could be a memory that goes back to school years. In everyday life you will want to find some sort of short cut to reach a destination, either because you will be late for work or there is a will to be nifty, to try to make things easier. In all aspects you will see this. These are just some basic examples that have come upon us.

Having a look and thinking of progresses in society, there has been grand evolutions, where the human being has and always will try to make life easier. The mind, the needs and the effort bring these results That is why there have been the inventions that has bought about innovations. There are too many to mention at the moment but along the way we will be able to refer many.

The above expresses a sample of human nature and how it could function.

When somebody faces something that turns out to be complicated or puzzling, by nature that somebody may go about trying to find solutions, while another somebody cannot be bothered to puzzle itself.

Many people can find life too easy, others too hard. Nature always presents a bilateral situation. There is no "one way ticket" in any life time. There are challenges for each and every being.

This is just the beginning of a book that will aim to explain aspects.

The human nature is always fascinating. The quest of an explanation is always intriguing.

As mentioned before, Psychoanalysis is a challenge. As a therapist, I have able to observe plenty of situations. Any person does not have to be a therapist or a scholar to be able understand ideas that evolve from this. Psychoanalysis is not only just a plain term. It can be a part of life, and indirectly can be a "balance" of the soul. Apart from the so called "classic" methods, there can be many ways to go about doing this, even if we ourselves analyze ourselves indirectly in everyday life with thoughts and memories, even using a simple everyday accessory that we haven't thought of using for something like this.

There will be a theoretical analysis in the fist stage of the book. Then there will be an account of some cases with the usage of the method and then a self guide of handling the method that can be done very easily.

CHAPTER

1

The every day challenge in life always will lead into situations. It always comes about in every day that we live. We will always think whether directly or indirectly on what will be ahead of us on the next day, as soon as we end our day and we go to sleep for example. There are the feelings and the result of the day, or it even could be a continuation of previous days and could have an expected continuation in the following days to come. A continuation of an issue can be around for a long time but it could stop somewhere either abruptly or by stages either with a solution or an event that will just stop the situation. This could be called the flow of life. We all face a flow of situations. There is no static situation in life. Things cannot be stopped. Problems will come about. Solutions will also come about.

Most of us have not come accustomed to review at the end of the day and to have a plan for the day coming in a practicing way. For most of us it comes naturally. For others practice has to come about.

These situations will have an influence on each person. There can be signs, whether they are physical or psychological. The effects will have physical and psychological impact that will show either directly or indirectly.

If the situation that comes about produces some sort of problem that could provide some sort of change, whether positive of negative, either with discomfort, then there are ways to face the situation directly or indirectly.

A consideration of being for each day is a usual function. Each person will look their being in a matter of seconds, after waking up from their sleep. This is a typical case here where somebody wakes up in the morning, because it could be in another part of the day considering if that person is on some sort of shift where the period of sleep will be different. From the sleep, it is possible to acquire some sort of dream. This could affect that person, and the influence of that dream could go on for the rest of the day, whether it would have been a good or bad dream.

Everyday life, or routine can be able to affect a person. Situations that mark a life style can mark a persons inner self. These effects can be seen from some people that will be expressive, whether they want to express themselves or either they do not want to show expressions and effects, but do show this. There will be a reference to these later on.

Lets consider ourselves on each start of our day. There is a function of the awakening and then we go about to do our normality. Each day is and will be different. A person could wake up to a good mood. Others not. Some will start of well. Some not. There will be the usage of everyday items that we take for granted. A normal routine. a beginning of the day.

Firstly waking up, going to the bathroom, washing showering, shaving(if a male), putting makeup(if female). A typicality. Things will vary, but it is a normal routine.

In the bathroom there is the faucet, the taps, and the mirror! You look at your face in the mirror. You see yourself in the mirror. Other people you face at the times of the day will see you, including your face. You do not see your face, unless you have a mirror to see the state your face is in. Your face can be a sign of what can be happening to you, apart from any sort of feeling you could be feeling at that moment.

The mirror is a humble everyday utensil that everyone uses both directly and indirectly. The aim of this book is about the usage of this humble utensil. On how we can use significantly. How we can be able to use the mirror fruitfully. The mirror can show someone more things to that person, that other people will not probably see.

The mirror is a fascinating tool for everyone. The mirror is used in many ways. It is there and many of us haven't really figured out why is a mirror there for. The best way a mirror is used, is to be used wisely.

We can use the mirror for therapeutic matters in Psychology. It can even provide an excellent tool for Psychoanalysis. It is not a method of "self psychoanalysis" because a person cannot really do much without guidance from a trained and skilled therapist. This is where any problem comes about. This will be observed.

All situations come out from a cause that will always be detected. Whether it will take a short period of time, or a long time. Causes will leave their mark indirectly or directly. These are the basic principles of any type of therapy, that does include Psychoanalysis.

All of us have practiced this in some indirect way.

The needs of everyday life brings this up. A start of the day, as soon as somebody wakes up to start off the day will always have something to do. The total basic human functions will be in working order. A person that is inert, lethargic, not active, feeling down, has something that comes about from a cause. The causes of this, mainly depression, stress, comes about either from the basic everyday life, where there are negative effects that brings about these results.

Depending on the situation, a person's disposition will be acquired for the day that is to be faced.

Normality for each person will be relevant. No normality is carbon copied. Every person functions differently. That is why people are individuals. Behavioral patterns differ as well for each person. Environments may be similar but each person will differ.

All are taken into account when we see each case when the individual will seek therapy. The individual will know best on the beings self. Therapy will be the helping hand when needed.

Let us look at a typical day for someone. The person will wake up after a period of rest, that is sleep. Usually in the morning, whether early, whether later on in the morning. After getting out of bed, a person will usually do a routine. A person will realize that it is the day of the week that has been awoken to. Let's say Monday. Automatically that person will realize that it is the start of the week, and typicality will lead the person to the normality of that day. So the person will go about getting ready to face the day in the best way possible. The same will happen for Tuesday, Wednesday, Thursday, Friday and then the weekend, Saturday and Sunday. If at work, that person will prepare for the day. Usually there will be a day or two where that person will stay at home and not go to work.

At work the needs and demands each day are different. Schedules are set for each day. Each person will be influenced by this. Dispositions come from this. Stress and depression will also come about when a person cannot handle uncomfortable situations. There are expected situations for each day, but there are also unexpected situations. This is where there are imbalances come about and this is where a person can be able to handle this situation. These imbalances bring effects to the mental well being that can also affect the physical well being and will exhibit some psychosomatic situation that will be uncomfortable.

The mirror here can be used by the person for the observation of the situation. An effect of any sort will be clear. The person may be afraid to see this. Many can even overuse the mirror and in no significant way.

So, a typical day will start off normally and typically. Each day will have its routine, its errands, its obligations. The mirror will help us see our composure in getting ready for work, in going to the work place, in going to a function, an appointment, on how we will dress, how we will groom, on how we will make ourselves and be decent enough for a society. If a person is not groomed and in scruffy, or if there is a problem in the makeup for example, there will be strange reactions from others in a society. Without the help of a mirror, it is hard to do this.

The mirror is also a tool for many occupations. Tailors will use the mirror to help out in the measurements and the cuttings of the fabric. Hairstylists have the mirror for the haircuts, beauty parlors will use the mirror extensively The dentist will use a dental mirror to see the teeth in the mouth, for example. There will be plenty of uses as well.

More will be seen in the following chapters where there will be references to the mirror with everyday situations without being specific at first. This will come later. But remember this. This is just a guide of the usage of the mirror that will help us in other things that many have not considered yet.

CHAPTER

2

In a typical day, we will be able to see ourselves many times in a mirror. It is generally a routine. Apart from the bathroom where there will be a standard mirror, in many houses there will be a mirror placed at somewhere else. Consciously or not the mirror is always used, in plenty of ways. The mirror can be used excessively. The image seen in the mirror shows us an everyday picture of ourselves.

This has been with us from the beginning of our lives. Well at least from the beginning of those early days in our lives that we can remember today. A child will see an image of itself in the mirror and will start to get curious. The child will be fascinated with the mirror. Every person is always curious right from the beginning.

A child will consider the mirror as a game, and will always be fascinated with the image seen. In later periods of life, a male child will probably mimic his father, and the female child will mimic her mother. An older sibling can be mimicked as well. It will be considered rare that a child would want to mimic some person of the opposite sex. This shows primary behavioral tendencies. Behavior usually acquired from an environment. The behavioral patterns expresses the way in which somebody can function. The mirror is there for someone to see all this.

The mirror shows change. From childhood to Adulthood. A person will see the image of their being in periods of life, where the person will be the first to know what is going on. The natural reactions of our being comes about. The reactions can be positive or negative. A person will either like the changes, but there can be people that will not like changes and will always want to remain the same. These reactions can be relevant. This awareness is visually depicted to a person with a mirror or from mirror like surfaces.

The mirror depicts a total composure of a person in general. The person will feel things from within, but at first will not really know what is going on, will get to see how this situation can be visually, when any person will see his composure from the mirror. These manifestations of the situation in other words, will make that person see things in detail. The feeling may not be intense, but there can be a mark showing a situation. A pimple on the face, for example can be troublesome for someone that can be worrying. That person will then try to think of ways of getting rid of that pimple. If that person is too self conscious then there can be a state of panic that can come about. Of course there is no need to panic. A solution will come about. Quick thinking and previous knowledge is always useful to overcome the situation.

In the case of pain, a headache for example, the mirror can show a person that is suffering something of the like. Any type of head pain, whether it is a toothache or a migraine, the discomfort will also be visible, let alone feeling this. The mirror here makes things vivid.

The mirror is used many times a day without really realizing the amount of usage a day. The bathroom is used many times. For personal grooming, to wash hands, a person will see himself in the mirror many times a day. This can be useful. There is always a feeling of self improvement at some stage. This depends on the self consciousness. People can tend to overuse the mirror, some seem to avoid the mirror because they can tend to see things and not like what they see. Both extremities are questionable. A balance is perfect to be achieved.

No one can't avoid the mirror. Unless there are no mirrors in the place somebody lives in. There is always an object that will depict somebody's reflection though. There are ways of handling all types of situations. As each person is different, each person will use and see the mirror from their point of view. This can be seen from the stages of life. From the infantile stage to the elderly stage we have seen our changes. We have seen the ways of different usage. We will be able to see ways in the chapters that follow.

CHAPTER

3

The usage of the mirror is made to be simple. There are no complexities. As mentioned, the mirror is used by us in various ways. The psychological state of each person can make a difference in the use of the mirror. Environmental influences can bring about many characteristics of people on how they function. This is how each situation is faced. From a normal acquaintance, a meeting, to facing the mirror for use in whatever way will have its reasoning.

The usual use is for us to see how we are and how we will be able to face a situation. Others will use the mirror simply because there is a fascination with whatever will be seen, whether the image seen by us liked or not. This is where the self assessment is recognized. We call it empathy. It is our self cognition. This is where we see what is going on. We also see and feel how a sense is associated with the way we will look with some situation, if a feeling is directly connected. We have rare cases where the outer look doesn't have any relationship with an inner feeling.

All of the above is somewhat general. All people are unique. This is where we all have the different usage. These first parts will try to explain the many situations when we all face the mirror.

Women will usually use the mirror more than men. The routine of putting the makeup, that takes a while will be time consuming compared to a man that will shave, or either to trim face hair whether it is either a moustache, a beard or both.

A female will tend to know the mirror better than the male. A female tends to be more familiar to the mirror than a male. It is probably a part of a female nature. The female tends to have a stronger tendency that seems to be advanced. The male on the other hand seems that tendency is less.

It is also the culture of every person, the way somebody will be bought up, the environments as well are able to form the various behaviors that are known to us and how it is formed. A role for a female and a male can be established. This is where a normality is formed. A typical normal behavior. If there is a change in habits in general, well that is another story.

Empathy comes early. The mirror can fascinate people at an early age. People will get conscious toward the mirror. Any person of normal being, that is of a normal sound mind will not be "at war" with the mirror. The mirror could even become a friend for someone. It can also turn out to be an enemy if a distortion of the mind can be observed. We will come to that later.

How is it so that the mirror can be useful to us at an early age, even though it will take time for us to understand what is a mirror. It will start off as a game. A child will see its image as a reflection and will probably wonder what is the child seeing?

I remember my first experiences with the mirror, where I saw myself as an image in front of me. What am I seeing?... I would have said, I would have thought in my infantile mind. As a family friend of ours told me when she was baby sitting me, she said that I was looking at the mirror, I see the image of myself, I thought that it was a real life person and I wanted to reach out and touch that person that I was seeing in the mirror. I was explained later on what was going on. A similar first experience of the mirror exists for many people. The young mind is fascinated with the reflection. It has been mentioned by many friends of mine, but also with many situations when I ask people the certain question when in session.

The mirror will then get to be a part of us. It will be a part of a person's toy. The image from the mirror can be an imaginary friend, where that reflection from the mirror can get to be a friend. Consciousness is born here, because the inner self will communicate with the outer self. The mirror can help here! In the stages of life we will all see all these uses, even though this skill will become acquired. Empathy is natural for all. The way in which it is used will become acquired.

The experiences are plenty with these first influences.

As the so called discovery comes to us naturally, the so called "driving forces" come within the environment. The child will see the parent of the same sex doing things, by using the mirror. The parent is usually the first direct role model for the child so there is a tendency o mimicking.

A young boy will see his father shave and look at himself dressing, and how he dresses. There will be a tendency of copying. A young girl will see the mother dressing herself and putting on the make up.

Similar mimicking will come about at school, in the early years. In Pre School and in the early years of Primary School, a part of play was "dress ups". This was where old garments were given to the school so that children could play around. It was an adventure for us the young children then to dress up like our fathers, or mothers, or like other grown ups. The situation was even funnier when young boys put dresses on, and the girls dressed up as men…Now there can be a topic for further discussions, having to do with choice.

In later years with more consciousness, there is plenty of experimentation. A female will tend to have more of a need to look at the mirror seeing herself. In the years of puberty, the changes are observed in both males and females. The females tend to be more self conscious. The males tend to "run late" with the need of seeing themselves changing and looking good and seeing how they are. A female will generally look at herself even more. The male will get conscious when something will come up in his life and he sees that he has to attract and look good. A female will look and see how she will develop and becomes more self conscious. All with the help of the mirror. Nothing of this kind can't be done without the help of the mirror.

In the situation of depression, a person will not want to look at himself. The inner feeling within the soul is horrible. The need of looking at the mirror image won't be necessary to that person. Depression comes about from many situations. Either there is a major disappointment that can't be faced and no solution comes about. The influence will be obvious and it will affect that person.

The mirror reflection is a sign of what can go about. Something that will be seen, but not felt will be obvious. The face grimaces are signs where the mirror shows what is going on. This is where reluctancy comes about with the fear of facing situations. From theories and from observations conclusions can come about. Although there are infinite answers. The search is always here.

A person is curious by nature there are discoveries every moment. People are not accustomed to search reasons. The mirror works in such situations, even though many people can't see how things can happen and how clear can something become with the use of the mirror.

CHAPTER

4

Before going on to see how the mirror can be used for other main reasons let us see what a mirror can do with the way we see images, how we can see the images and how would we like to see things in the mirror.

The mirror shows us what we see. We would probably like to see ourselves differently in the way we want to see ourselves, but the mirror shows us what we do see.

We would probably like to see ourselves with an image that can be ideal to us. A male would like to see himself more "handsome" and to be able to make a woman want this man to be "God's gift to women". Something like that can be considered by a woman, by considering herself "God's gift to man"! The imperfect characteristics can be seen and that person can face up to them. Seeing the face first, the imperfect features can be blemishes that can ruin any image. A wrinkle or two can ruin this image as well. This can also depend on age or on ways where a person can retain a complexion that can be perfect. The wrinkle on a face, on skin in various parts of the body can depend on age an on the way of life that can bring this about. Of course there are ways to cover this. Women will be more prone to cover this by the amount of makeup used. Men seem not to use as much makeup in general terms but there are series of products for men that can be makeup..

The body composition is also significant. A woman will see herself with a very attractive body and will feel competent. A man can be feeling like that along the same line when he sees that all is well.

In the case of obesity, where some parts will be full of body volume that will bring about abnormality with the symmetry of the body will make the person, either male or female feel uncomfortable of themselves. This is where solutions can come about.

Exercise and a balanced diet do help out in the way a body will be able to go into an ideal form. The collection of excess in any body depends on how that person is. Men usually have the belly. Women will have lower parts of the body. The posterior, the thighs for example. Women will probably have a situation with the breasts. The sizes are relevant depending on how the woman wants them. Tight and perky are the ideal breasts. The size is relevant, in the way of thinking, all depending on how the total body can be with the height and weight. For the males it is mainly the muscle tone. Men usually are more physical, they exercise, their actions need to be more energetic. Others can have muscle tone without any real effort. Others can put in plenty of effort. It is the way of life in which each person follows. Many people will want an ideal image without effort.

There may be many imperfect features in the face, Apart from the rinkles and the blemishes that can come about easier, imperfect points could be cosmetic. For people that are sensitive there are rectifications, e.g Rhinoplasty, Orthodontics, Otoplasty, and the classic facelifts of course.

A person that can be sensitive and vigilant can do all this. Firstly being cautious, needing outside help if needed. A person not being to self conscious either will have depression issues where that person will never give a damn about his or her being, and the image of the mirror will not make that person self conscious.

All of this will combine in how the exterior look will be and how can someone show how the being is on the outside. Of course this is consciousness. How a person wants to dress will make that person look and feel better and comfortable

The mirror can show this and will show many more things that can be detected.

CHAPTER

$$\boxed{5}$$

By looking at a mirror each day, a person will able to see the changes and the progression of the self. From childhood to puberty and adolescence and then adulthood, that is in stages. From the young maturity to old age. The advantages and the disadvantages. How some person retains the being. How does age results in this. How that person can retain things and not needing to use additives to make the self retainable. A male can see himself lose hair or grey at some stage. The wrinkles are an issue with both males and females, along with the grey hair. Loss of teeth can be an issue.

As for styles, that depends on the moods. Women can dye their hair to a color that will suit them. Men do this as well, but it is not a usual practice. Men can add on facial hair by growing a moustache, a beard, or both. Men will want to see themselves this way. Women will want to change their hairstyles, to comb their hair differently. Men will do the same, but Women are more prone to be sensitive with beauty aspects. We did mention in the previous chapter about this, by wanting to improve their so called imperfections. The mirror will give them help in seeing this and by using the mirror, they can be able to go about "rectifying" a situation.

Many people are scared of the mirror, when they will see themselves in a situation that they do not want to see. This fear will be overcome.

The mirror can be therapeutic in many ways as well. By looking at the self for a couple of minutes, that person will face someone very familiar and they can be able to talk to that image. We will get into this in later chapters because this procedure seems to be useful for situations.

The mirror will be used to depict the image a person wont be able to see without the help of the mirror. The image without the mirror will seem to be imaginary and the imaginary image will not be the factual image that is depicted in real life.

Many things cannot be done without the help of the mirror and many occupations will be dependent on the mirror to see things better. There will be a referral to this in the next chapter.

The mirror does give a better and more detailed picture of a situation having to do with the self. If a person is able to grasp the empathy needed and required at that moment, the mirror helps on many things. We will see them in the following chapters.

CHAPTER

6

Looking at the previous chapters, for starters we realize that the mirror can be used for a wide range of purposes, and not just the basic uses many have not really understood the depth of the mirror and its uses. Applications of the like will be mentioned in the next chapters.

The mirror, an obvious tool, is used in many professions. For many professions it is a desperate need. For other professions, the mirror makes the work easier and will put more detail.

The hairdresser, or barber along with a beautician will use the mirror extensively in their work. The mirror makes things easier for them to apply their art. The hairstyle or the beauty secrets applied towards their customers makes things better for them. It makes the customers look better, and seeing the end results will make the customers feel better with the result seen, The imperfections are supposed to be improved. The applied result wont go astray and it will not be based on chance but on whatever they know in their ability. This can be also done when a hairdresser can be avoided and the person can execute a hairstyle by him or herself. The mirror provides the image needed to guide a person to a required result, and not to do this without any guidance in the way of cutting the hair. There can be a person within the family or in a close environment that can be able to provide someone a haircut. That person needs the mirror for that guidance as well. Makeup and beautician skills can be applied by someone at home of course with the use of the mirror.

The makeup artists at television stations for the productions of television programs and the makeup artists with theatres or cinema sets will also use the mirror in their dressing rooms to prepare the actors are also included here.

Clothing can be tried on with the use of the mirror, either at the fashion shop or the clothing store or at home of course. The clothing stores have a space for someone to try clothing on. In that changing room there is a mirror so that the person trying on the clothing can see the image of the clothing when worn by the person. This is where there can be changes and altercations if there are to be any. This can also be happening at home if clothing bought at a fashion store wasn't been tried on at the store.

For the basics, when a person doesn't know what to wear for a certain day, that person can choose some clothing and looking at the mirror has the chance to play around with the combination of clothes up until the final decision. All with the help of the image seen from the mirror.

The use of the mirror can be seen in gymnasiums and at sporting centers. These include Dance Schools, Martial Arts Clubs, and Fight Clubs, just to name a few sporting venues that can use the mirror extensively.

Dance schools teaches its students movement. In practice the full scale mirror is there for the student to look at him or herself on how the movement comes out and how the movement is applied, and how each move is done. The mirror does help here and it is an excellent guidance tool. A similar situation is applied with Fight clubs when the athlete will see himself (or herself) with the movement. This can be continued at home. This practice was very useful during the Covid 19 quarantine procedures a couple of years ago when no one was allowed to move about freely, when the gymnasiums and Fight clubs were closed. To keep up with the fitness and to not lose track then, all instructors advised their student followers to do these procedures.

We will not forget older technologies with cameras and photographic methods where the mirror was used. Today there are methods having to do with digital technology, leaving the mirror aside.

Medicine in general has tools that have the mirror as a basis. The mirror is a tool that can give an in depth observation directly and indirectly.

Dentists use the mirror intensively. A dentist's most important tool for examination is the dental mirror. Observations are difficult with the inner teeth of a person without this. Dentists have tools that are based on the mirror. We only probably know about the dental mirror, but there are other important tools based on the mirror as well.

A mirror is important with other aspects of medicine. Many parts of the body are difficult to examine with the naked eye. ENT specialists use tools based on the mirror.

Physiotherapists use the mirror to see the movement of the patient after basic treatment. The professional can see the movement without the mirror, but ths does help the patient see progress in the therapeutic procedure

Psychologists/Psychiatrists will tend to use the mirror as a indirect therapeutic means. It is not applied as much as it should be. A reference of these uses will follow in the following chapters.

CHAPTER

7

The mirror is not used "officially" by the Psychologists to help out with mental health issues. The mirror is used to help out further with assumptions. Issues come about from the classic method of the dialogue with interviews between the therapist and the patient/client. The assumptions made either by the therapist, by the patient/client or by both parties will help out in the situation when it will come about. The patient/client can be able to see the condition of his or hers disposal. If there is a expression that is good enough to help the therapist come about with solutions, the work of the therapist will be easier.

The mirror gives the opportunity to make a person know oneself just by talking to him/herself at the mirror only for a couple of minutes. It will start a search within the inner self.

Many people probably had found it difficult to express themselves in front of a group of people. The mirror does help to overcome some sort of nervousness. It provides an excellent practice before a speech in front of people. Actors/actresses may use the method as a part of a successful rehearsal, before going about appearing on stage or on the television set if there is a taping of a show.

The mirror is used for practices as well. Speech therapists will use the mirror when the emphasis of speech to a person that is cared for will see the way the speech is correct from the mirror. The person that undergoes speech therapy will see how the lips, tongue and teeth will move to pronounce the correct word and the further practice helps the person to overcome that impairment.

The self dialogue is very important and very effective using the mirror. It only takes a couple of minutes at least so that the person can be able to see what is going on with that person. The mirror can be a close friend to somebody. It can make that person reveal oneself and not hide within the person's self.

People wanting to hide an imperfection can't do so with the mirror. The mirror provides solutions on any improvements to make oneself look better, feel better to function better. Observation is the main factor here, so that there can be a "guide" for each person to make things better for each person that will adopt a personal way of using the mirror.

The way of using the mirror is a personal situation. There are no "standard" procedures. Most of us just use the mirror because it is there, but using the mirror wisely can bring about results that you just cannot imagine.

The following chapters will refer to patients that used the mirror in such ways where more results, from the so called expected results have been assumed.

Just remember, this is not "the cure". It will be the beginning of the search for solutions and for functioning, in avoidance to issues that will probably would have made simple things harder.

CHAPTER

The following chapters will have to do with applications having to do with theories. The theory becoming applicable is a magnificent experience. For many it is just an event. For therapists this can be significant. The findings are useful. The quest for further investigation can become exciting.

Observation is significant for any therapist. Empathy is significant when the causes can be tracked down.

Therapeutic procedure with psychological issues is different to that of standard medicine. Standard medicine has observation, as with all medicine, a diagnosis follow and then the procedure of a cure is either with an inventional method followed on with a medicinal regime.

The methods in Psychiatry are different with diagnoses. The main tool is empathy, after observation. The therapeutical method has a series of sessions where the therapist will adjust the patient/

client to new standards. It is wise to avoid drugs. Drugs do help but they do not provide the "cure" as with causes of standard medicine. There is no panacea in Psychiatric medicine. People will have to abide with a situation.

Psychological situations are not due to a virus or a bacterium for example. There are other ways of influence that brings up s situation. A situation can be bought about by an environmental factor, whether it is direct or indirect. The way of life is also a factor. Every moment matters with things that can happen at any moment.

Depending on how each person can function, that person will be in the position of being affected directly or indirectly. When we say directly, a situation can provoke an immediate reaction that can cause a person to get upset. If that situation does not cause immediate reactions, it will probably do so after a while. This effect can cause a regression after a long time. That comes up when something happens and instead of doing something at a certain moment, does not happen. The yearn may come about many years later, when all is too late.

Where does the mirror fit into all of this? This is how…

The first thoughts came with a patient/client many years ago, when starting counselling. Simple things are so obvious but we cannot determine them at that moment.

The patient/client did mention about observations seen in the mirror. My observation went along the lines to the disposition. The therapeutic method was established.

45 year old male. Caucasian. Recently divorced(then), unemployed(then). The job situation was significant for him and

with finding a job was hard work by itself. He was realizing that problems were going to come about. The only financial support was the unemployment benefit. This situation made him feel upset and was in a bad disposition. His friends were nit available, so that he could go about and talk to somebody, to get things off his chest. All thoughts and ideas were bottled up inside him. He didn't want to do anything. He felt stressed. He got edgy for no apparent reasons apart from the situation that has come about. Even with his search for a new job made him feel depressed. Nothing was going right for that person. He felt like he was drowning into his depression.

At first he didn't want to do anything. He then saw that nothing is going right, and advice from a friend he was able to get in contact told him to go about and fight to survive. He started to feel the notion to go about and look at life. He said to himself that, this is going nowhere. He saw himself in the mirror whenever he felt like seeing himself in the mirror and he didn't like what he saw. At that stage he was always considering to avoid looking at the mirror. His complexion was not at its best. He didn't watch his diet. Apart from his smoking habit that increased, he had a tendency of overdrinking This was just a sample of his depression. He lost his self esteem. He was an introvert. Due to his closed character, he felt difficulty in expression.

There were two options. Since he was religious, he considered that the Church would provide him with aide and with a solution to his problem. Confession played a major part with him and the parish priest would keep confidentiality and felt comfortable in speaking to him, since he knew him from his youth. With confession he felt somewhat better. This was not enough. The priest told him that for further scientific advice, and if there has been a problem that has come about, then it would be wise to go and see a therapist. The clergy does not think positively of "spiritual" therapy in many parts of the world. But that is another story...

With reluctance the patient/client came to me after an appointment, where he was able to become expressive and started telling me his story. He started to be confused and I asked him that his expression should be in a rational sequence. He was able to concentrate and put things in order. I did help him with this expression flow. I did understand him with his nervousness. With the priest he was comfortable. I had to make him feel comfortable to make my job easier. For somebody to face a therapist for the first time, it is like that person is in a vehicle and doesn't know how to drive it. This is where a therapist through conversation makes him drive the vehicle by him/herself and trying to get out of a "emotional maze".

Step by step this person was starting to slowly regain his self esteem. With all the disappointments he faced at that period of time, he lost himself. He was on the verge of a serious and tragic mental state. He felt it was time that he needed help. That is why he went for help to his nearby clergyman, because he was taught this way. He was trying to solve his problem by himself. For someone to go to a therapist, a personal decision is needed. Even though it can be recommended by others, if the decision isn't taken up by that same person, that person cannot be pushed to do this. This is where a certain problem lingers on if there is no decision for serious help. Problems can be easy to solve here, and the therapist is not needed. A direction is needed though.

When the patient/client was able to put things in order and started to express himself in the way that will lead him to solutions, things became better. Help became easier. Solutions came about.

He would go on to say, "I saw myself in the mirror while I was washing my face, and I looked at myself and I felt like I hated myself, because I was a failure. Everything was not going well for me! I am unemployed. I have no partner. I am alone. Nobody wants me!"...

I will reply, "That is not the case! This is just a testing period that people will have at some stage". The thing that I heard was something that I liked and was surely useful for future needs. We were able to obtain a tool.

Life in general is a continuous "war" of survival. We will have to establish friends that will help us against the enemy. In this case, a simple mirror will be our friend. The use will be significant.

The target here is to make sure we reach goals. Each situation that is needed to be solved has facts and has aims. We will have to think simply to reach a solution. The mirror here can help.

Just with a couple of minutes of serious conversation with yourself using the mirror, this can help us bring the problem about. This is where the quest for a solution comes about. Work has to be done by the patient/client. The therapist will just guide here. Each situation is different. There may be common factors, with many situations, but each situation is different. Solutions have to be "tailor made" for each person. Every individual is different.

The individual has to "own up" with him/herself, no matter the cost and no matter on how things really are.

There have been situations with many people when they haven't "owned up" with the real truth where they wished things would have turned out along with their thought, while in reality, things did not happen like that. In our case, we were lucky that there weren't any fantasies. Things would have become more complicated here, and no solution would have come about.

Our patient/client here did cooperate tin the best possible way and we got results. Things became better for him and it turned out that it was just a period of crisis in his life. The results did not come quickly. There was a certain period of time where there was a application of the exercises that helped out in the end. There was a reluctance at first. There was a lot of hard work. The results came out. At first he was going to give up. He did mention though that he was looking at the mirror. He had some degree of depression. He was wanting medication to face up to the depression. A mild tranquilizer was given to him and it would have been used at moments that the depression was uncontrollable. With simple deep breathing exercises, the depression crises were faced. The use of the mirror wasn't new to him. The environment that he grew up in did help out where he was shown how to use the mirror by his parents. Moral help and support came up in turn.

CHAPTER

9

It was mentioned that Psychiatry has no "magic wand" and no panacea for the "cure", as with standard medicine where with certain medications, the therapy comes about, from the common cold to the most complex conditions.

The way in which a certain condition is faced is always different. This is how guidance comes about.

In the previous chapter our patient/client was stricken with a number of problems with his situation. It was made possible for him to come about with solutions and he was fortunate that things came out in a satisfactory situation.

He was able to find a job after a period of constant and vigorous searching. He was desperate in seeking for a job. A job meant survival for him. It was difficult to find a job with his age. He did fear a very long period of unemployment.

He did overcome his degree of shyness. There was a lack of self esteem. For every interview, he "rehearsed" in front of the mirror so that he could work on his general appearance and presentation

He was able to find a "significant other", after a while, when he least expected it. He was able to see a "weakness" here. It seemed for him that he was in a quest for a certain type of partner. It turned out that by trying "something else" with a partner, that this choice did turn out to be harmonious for him. How was he able to recognize a weakness?

Just after his divorce, along with all the ills happening in his life then, he emotionally locked out everything. He didn't want anything. He was able to start feeling free with his choices when he started being "on the prowl". He saw his weakness. He had a conversation with himself. He saw his strengths and his weaknesses in his approach. His significant other came about when waiting at the bus stop. A conversation came about. The continuation came later. He couldn't believe that there was this significant other so close to him and he did not see how close this was.

This is just one of many examples of the general use of the mirror in cases.

Each case has to be considered differently. The criteria, the needs are different. The quest for solutions are always there where each aspect can be significant for this.

CHAPTER

10

So we have reached the end with a basic account in the use of the mirror. This conclusion will lead us with thoughts on how we can use the mirror.

I just remembered that the mirrir is a basic factor that we can even face in childhood. Since we can be able to see the mirror and can be fascinated by this in early years, because we do get fascinated by this, we get to be taught with the uses of the mirror and we get to see how the mirror is used in early ages,

If we can recall the fairytale "Snow White and The Seven Dwarves" ,the classic phrase "Mirror Mirror on the Wall, who is the Fairest of them all?" is always remembered by everybody that has read the book or has heard the fairytale at a young age. Fairytales and myths from various civilizations have referred to the mirror in many ways where a young person will face the concept of the mirror.

We see that many basic "tools" are presented to us in ways indirectly so that it can express the importance of something like the mirror. There will have to be another book about the myths and the fairytales that will talk about basic factors faced by people in later life.

With our referral here with the uses. This is also a basic use that is historical. This fairytale goes back in time. Similar stories can be referred by us in our memories.

A case like the one presented are many. The many cases bring about different results, but remember these results go along the line of the basic aim in each case. Many different cases can be referred.

Just remember that the mirror can be a very useful tool and when used wisely can bring about results wanted.

Therapeutic processes guides the person to further good use if the mirror when factors are there and when the aims will be achieved. Everything is a challenge. A solution to the situation comes about. Nothing comes automatically. There may be catalysts that will help out and make things easier. But if there is no cognition of the situation, if the signs seen from the mirror are not seen, then you can't do nothing. The aim achieved is the ideal situation each person puts into application. This has to be believed, and the person has to live it. If there is superficial thinking, the aim will not come about but the initial situation will just remain

www.ingramcontent.com/pod-product-compliance
Lightning Source LLC
Chambersburg PA
CBHW031238120626
46545CB00003B/1181